GLIMPSES

GLIMPSES

A MEMOIR IN POETRY

CAROL GREVER

DENVER, COLORADO

ACKNOWLEDGEMENTS

I wish to acknowledge with gratitude the encouragement, intellect and keen ear of my friend, Dr. Eleanor Hubbard. Our weekly meetings to share our writing efforts helped hone these poems into a full length book. She is a true friend.

Versions of some of these poems have appeared in other publications and are included in this collection with permission. Publications include *From the Heart* (Beth N. Davis, ed); *I Love You All Day* (Philip Dacy and Gerald M. Knoll, ed.); *Contemporary Christian Poets* (Virginia Mollenkott, ed.); *Memory Quilt, The Haymaker; Ram's Horn, Unity Magazine; Boulder Camera; Images; Oklahoma English Bulletin; Christianity and Literature; and Soliloquy.*

Outskirts Press, Inc.
http://www.outskirtspress.com

ISBN: 978-1-4327-8939-8

Outskirts Press and the "OP" logo are trademarks belonging to Outskirts Press, Inc.

PRINTED IN THE UNITED STATES OF AMERICA

ALSO BY CAROL GREVER

Nonfiction

My Husband Is Gay
A Woman's Guide to Surviving the Crisis

When Your Spouse Comes Out
A Straight Mate's Recovery Manual

Memoir

Memory Quilt
A Family Narrative

Poetry

Sun of a New Dawn

For Dale

CONTENTS

PREFACE

This is a history of sorts, glimpses into a long life informed by reading and writing. After more than seven decades on this earth, my vitality hasn't waned, but the ending of this story is inevitable. It is time for a reckoning, an examination of ultimate meaning. With deepest gratitude for this precious human life, it is time to mine the past to learn what it has taught. This collection of poetry may suggest those fine distinctions.

One might say that I have always been writing this book. The earliest poems were written in young adulthood, the rest through the following fifty years, often in response to evocative events or significant transitions. They reflect nuances of an ordinary life's pain, growth, discoveries, bliss, and essential lessons. They reveal secrets, focus values, and expose flashes of wisdom. All were re-appraised, many revised for this book, bolstered by new pieces written expressly for the collection.

Gathering my body of poetry was a joyous experience. It was archaeology of the soul, mining earlier insights in the light of present understanding. The process identified distinct personal stages, each with different significance. Individual poems depict spots of time that illuminate vivid moments or mundane experience to afford insight through distilled meaning. Particular interests and longings appeared and changed. Mistakes chastened. Crises struck, love healed. Forgiveness brought recovery, and meditation brought serenity. Together, the poems offer brief glimpses of a life edging toward an end with acceptance and peace.

It was intriguing to take a step back to follow the flow of this single life through identifiable phases, demonstrated by poems written in all its seasons. It is my fervent wish that their themes may seem familiar to readers, evoking shared thoughts and experience.

Carol Grever

GENERATIONS

GENERATIONS

Hen-and-chicks
a common plant,
terra-cotta pot packed,
brimming with
mother and children
green babies galore.

A clumsy stumble
shakes their calm.
Trip on the step
drop the pot
bruise, shatter
the mother-plant.

Broken leaves drop
but roots survive
new plants thrive
proliferate.
oddly like the old,
but fresh.

Dying to live
survival comes
only with pain.

COVENANT

Larkspur float high in a lake of grass
violet blooms washed by waves of weeds.
An ancient walnut tree
guards a sag of fence.
Scattered bricks, broken walls:
Remnants of yesterday.
Beyond bare ruin
is a past that is part
of now's reality.
Look into meanings
as through sunlit streams,
moments shining like smooth-washed stones—
polished monuments to a history of grief.

A house stood here
in this life-lost lot.
Wandering over rutted rubble
search for signs—
broken glass in morning-glory vines.
Out there was the road
two ruts of hot red dust
printed with stinging bare feet,
Three children
padding up cinder block steps
racing to the high yard
shady and cool.
The pounded dirt path
ignored a cracked sidewalk,
both reaching for the wide porch.

Summer was best
with flowers everywhere—
in pots and broken bowls
in tubs and buckets
in the diamond-shaped fishpond
paved with water lilies.
There was mint to sniff and chew
deep green leaves smelling of coolness,
pink honeysuckle to pluck
for its drop of sweet,
fuchsia four-o'clocks
hanging heavy by the fence,
and Grandpa's favorite larkspur
waving all around.

The house was huge and old
smelling of must and age and warmth,
rich with child-treasure.
The tattered screen banged shut
behind rushing youngsters
oblivious of woe within.
There by those weeds
is the place where the hall was.
There was the closet
full of old coats and purses
ready for pretending and penny-hunts.
There was the heart-shaped pin cushion
just above the drooping rocker.
All the chairs had holes and cracks—
veterans of long combat
in other people's houses.
But they still would do
for Saturday nights of "Grand Old Opry."

3

The living room had rose-printed wallpaper
and pictures of family
kept warm by the puffing gas stove.
Other rooms were mostly unused
but here was the bedroom
long and light
filled with beds and chests
boxes and baskets
sewing machines and gadgets.
Grandpa was here
all that time he was sick.
The smell of that sickness
lingers
after all the operations.
His yellowed skin and wrinkled hands
made him a stranger
to seven-year-old eyes.

But his well days are clearer—
soft hair and rusty black suits,
"Old Dan Tucker" sung
in droning monotone,
rocking away hours
in the chair with the comforting squeak.
There were breakfasts
in the kitchen,
red-checkered oil cloth shining
under plates of biscuits and gravy.
There was sorghum and butter
mixed in a puddle
to drip down small chins.
The stove stayed warm all day
for fried apple pies and dumplings and greens,

making much of little.
Making much of little—
like the canary caged
by the window
you, Grandma, sang.
And the children learned.
But the lessons are only now real.
Your sweet humility when you'd say,
"I've not swept today,"
looking at the dusty floors.
Your lace collars fastened with a pin,
your soft wrinkled face,
your gray mottled hair
pulled back in braids
and wound like a halo:
You are real now to me.

The house is gone with your days
but you'll live as long
as I remember the trunk full
of childish delight
on your back porch—
Dress-up jewelry and old high heels.
You'll live as long
as I remember the days
when I'd rather have been at your house
than anywhere else in the world.

Looking around this mass of loss,
I see other days instead
and breathe a long goodbye.

FALLSCAPE

Chirr of cricket
Cicada drone
Wind in blackjack
Bird dog moan
Tree frog rhythm
Caw of crow
Laze of lizard
Ant-trail mow
Dry leaf rustle
Thunder's threat
Turbulent calm
Rain-scent wet:
Tulsa October.

THE POTTER, THE PARENT

You wedge clay first
prepare it to be:
knead out air-pockets
work away flaw-causes
the mass yet soft.

The wheel comes next.
Round and round,
experience repeated.
Unless the clay's centered
it'll never be true.
The pot fails that starts off balance.
Round and round, you mound it
But it's still not done.
It has to be useful too.

Skillfully, you open it
to new shapes,
thumbs in first
ease the friction
wet the clayey smoothness.
Gently! Too much pressure
and it's ruined.
Bring up the sides,
higher and higher.
(Sometimes it balks;
clay's independent!)
Build the cylinder
ever so slowly
and it takes
a form unique.

Round and round,
purpose evolves:
Its shape dictates
a future role--
a lamp, a bowl,
its destiny determined
by self-will grown
from the potter's hands.
You trim and glaze
but real creation's past.
No pot is perfect
But you approve with pride.
Content, you love it.

SPRINGSHINE

Sneakers creep to guard
his secret grin, half shy
under touseled blondness.
He holds behind him
Treasure.
 "Flowers, Mama."
Bright in his muddy fist
daffodil trumpets on tiptoed stems
harbingers of fluid warmth.
We share aware their glow
prepare to care and grow.
A gift of love to banish coldness
A gift of life to promise newness—
Springshine!

SPRING INTO SUMMER

Welcome
heat
birds
tweet
lambs
bleat
plants
complete
rows
neat
kids
meet
bare
feet
teams
compete
build
conceit
ice cream
treat
summer's
sweet

COMPLAINT

Old woman
daughter of some mother
were you young once?
Laughing without malice
smiling without sneer
pumping a race
feeling snow in your face?
Did you ever taste
your library paste?
Crave hot dogs and Hershey
hear music in noise?
Or stick out your tongue
at the grouch next door,
old woman?

TYPICAL TRIP
A Rondeau

The line forms here! Situation clear.
Vacation woe, bring up the rear.
You watch the clock, impatient pain
"Another wait" the trip's refrain.
Each minute seems to last a year.

To enter parks or buy a beer
or even view a winning steer,
kids start to whine, not just complain.
The line forms here!

We've come so far, paid prices dear
worked hard and long, locked in high gear.
We prayed for sun, but sloshed in rain.
The famous shows turned out inane.
Late flight for home, attendants sneer,
"The line forms here!"

AMUSEMENT PARK

Wasn't that great, Mom?
Just super, my love.
　　Though the seats
　　in that ride
　　fit my hips
　　like a glove.

The carousel next!
You show me the way.
　　And I'll pray
　　for a short ride
　　with sickness at bay

The fun house is scary!
I hid behind you!
　　And I yawned
　　when the zombie
　　reached out
　　with a boo!

Vacations with children
a parent's delight,
share innocent fun
but long for a flight

It wouldn't be worth it
but kissing goodnight
a sleepy, "Gee, thanks Mom,"
can make it all right.

VISITING ANGEL

Angels surround us
God's helpers disguised.
They might have
pink cheeks and pigtails,
stay for years, or just a day.
But we know
when they've touched us.

Who cares how many
can stand on a pinhead—
academic argument.
It takes only one,
laughing in play
asking hard questions
being so good
teaching us to be better,
to change our lives.

CONTINUANCE

Knotted face, too young for its frown,
an eight-year-old man
his hurt a magnet for yours
mirrored in your shaded eyes.
"I can't keep up."
Taut muscles, bitten nails
deepen his whisper.
You hold tighter
but arms aren't armor.
His face a likeness of yours
his hands, walk, hurt aren't new—
you've lived this before.
"They laughed at me,"
his muffled voice sighs
pressing on your heart.
Pajamaed legs
gangle over your knee
but for tenderness
a ludicrous pose.
How can you say,
he can, he will, he must
somehow.
Uncertainties change and soon
he'll hold another boy
with face too young to frown,
magnetic hurt
reliving his own.

MY CHILD

Watching you play
in placid waves
I ached
for your unevenness.
Sunset surf
laved sunburned legs
hobbling lamely.

Now you're a man.
Generation to generation
seen from a distance
tempered by age,
I view my own
imperfection.

I can't help you.

REMAINS

For my unborn grandchild

I dreamed of fragments
shattered pieces on the floor.
    Walk with care
    or you'll crush them!
A shard of crystal—
etched wine glass
cracked in mid-design.
Springs and casings
fittings and parts
once useful things
scattered and ruined
wrecked underfoot:
    Litter of life
    broken
like dreams
like my heart.

CENTRIPETAL

Miles of fields
ridges whiskered
with greening wheat,
landscape lulled
by layering hills.
From the highway
racing past phone poles
fence-posts counting off the miles,
it seems the world
is only wheat fields
and liquid sky.
That sky's so deep
the wonder is
the earth's not drowned.

Then ten miles on
a sheltering grove
varies the theme
of wheat and sky.
Among the trees,
a house,
small center
of someone's world.
Home.

Myopic, familiar
those passers of days
believe they pivot time,
miss the perspective
of a driver of highways,
rushing in space
to his own place—
The pivot
of course
of time.

HER WORLD

Quick, come look!
On tiptoe by the sink
she points to the curve
of Martin Circle.
See, there's the couple
from two doors down.
They walk their dogs
safe on leashes
but that cat of theirs
follows behind like a pup!
So cute,
looks proud and free.
Never saw a cat
people could take for walks.

Bender's got a new car
See in their drive?
They like it so far.
Nice color.

There's that little boy--
there in the cowboy hat--
he loves his red boots.
wears them every day.
His folks just moved
into Bonnie's place.
Poor Bonnie died so fast.
I miss her now.
Her kids threw away
all her stuff.
I saw them carry

load after load
to the dump.
About made me sick.

Wonder who's driving by so slow
looking at the house next door.
Wish it would sell.
There goes Roger now.
His big Malamute
tripped him on the ice.
His back still hurts.
Can tell the way he walks.

Mama stays busy
all day long
tracking her world
framed by the kitchen window.

TO BE OLD . . .

Flowers for Easter
from the church--
age revered by youth.

"Is that our kitty?"
Staring eyes, perhaps blind,
fill with fear.
"Is it all right? Is it all right?"
Anxious questions
in rolling eyes,
shuffling shoes.
"It's all right," I say
stroking her thin arm.
Slowing feet calm their pace.

A corner turned,
another row of chairs,
matchstick limbs gape
from drooping clothes.
Golden years graduates
nearing dust again
whispering, babbling
talking to people
not there.

Strongest among them
a wrinkled black granny
pushes her walker.
"Come shake my old hand, sonny."
Small white hand
wrapped in worn brown leather—

a moment.
Shining tears and peace.
"A sweet little hand!"
Her dry lips
touch his fingers
as he watches, awed,
learning what it is
to be old.

CALLING AND CAREER

TO TOUCH THE MOON

Small gray cloud
races, races
to touch the moon:
Serene dream
retreats endlessly.
Linking at last
cloud over moon
fresh illumination
lasting seconds.
Bright cloud
rushes on
racing, racing
back to gray
losing the light.

FINITUDE

Once upon a sometime
sometime in a nighttime
time writes lines on an age
for some.
And it sighs and cries
and needs and bleeds
but never lies
or dies.
You learn it too soon
or too late, that fate
which the half-knowing know
which the half-turned learn
or earn.
Born to be—but what?
Strive to do—but why?
Time's lines mine the truth
and finitude's a certitude.
The work and time last.
Man is mortal.

SUFFOCATION

Half a day's hunting's enough
when you're that young--
Dad went on alone.
Relieved, I rested,
retreated to book and backseat.
Thoreau's a good companion
in autumn pastures;
Walden was freedom
but pages grayed
as something stopped the sun.

Shapes all around
eyes looking through glass
front, back beside my ears,
eyes staring, broad noses pressing
moist lips champing yellow teeth.
Hundreds of eyes
surrounding suffocated screams.

Only cattle.
Their eyes seem kind,
yet terror knew no reason
in that rancher's field.

I still read Thoreau
see the sun stopped,
shapes gray my pages
as air clots with fear.
I hunt for escape
from eyes that demand
eyes that confront
eyes that condemn.
Freedom is lost when
those eyes smother it.

PEDAGOGIC

Beggarly, he grasps the days
Devours moments as a starveling.
So much to read and do:
Gobble, swallow facts
Slosh and slurp the hours
Drain the cups, lick the rims
No slowing
Suck the lees
Hurry!

Bloated and full
Drunk with haste
Sick with surfeit
Shamed with shallowness
Inebriate
He staggers to class
Stands before judgment
Jaded and worn, and
Vomits.

SKIMMING

Skim the surface!
It may suffice,
surfeit of cream,
no lean, until
glutted rich emptiness
reaches an edge
drops off the question
like a stone.
Even perfect rocks
drop in depth untested.
Flat perfection
skips waves lightly
but ultimately sinks.
Unreadiness drowns.
Successful seekers
learn to swim.
They dive alive.

OLD-TIME PROFESSOR

Flushed and spent, he forces
a last recalcitrant thought
into his mold.
"Ours at last," he gasps,
closing the cover
on his academic triumph:
Candidates for degrees,
scholars all, packed with facts,
minds enclosed in book-like form,
classified, shelved, complete,
uniform in all details,
row upon row, programmed--
defeated by discipline.

SONNET FOR A NEW DEGREE

Degrees, the recognition of the world
the full regalia academe bestows,
impressive caps and gowns like flags unfurled
inspired young dreams to make a decade glow.
Sophistic, ready to debate, defend
their hard-wrought wisdom proudly to the old,
disdaining time to try and test each trend,
too confident in self and theories bold.
Relentless time unscaled youth's guileless eyes
replacing joy with life's persistent pain
perspective clear to bring with wide surprise:
A scholar's knowledge is but hollow gain.
Time's cool and constant rule is this:
To walk God's path is peace and final bliss.

ONLY ONE?

My teacher said,
"To have one thing
you're good at
is enough."

Elusive quest
hard to discern
dilettante that I am.
I search.

One thing—
what one?
Dabble in
Writing, wifing
teaching, good works.
Play executive
mother sons
mend hurts
mind details
make small folks
feel big.

One thing—
What is the *one*
for commitment?
To have one is enough,
but I dream of the whole.

ON RESOLUTIONS

When I begin to write my wishes down
It seems the page holds insufficient space
For self-improvement lists I'll have to face
To earn my passage and attain my crown.
For miracles of wisdom, loss of hate
In each New Year false hope springs yet anew
But time reveals the realistic clue
That man is man; he can't himself create.
Without a God, lone efforts miss the mark
I need this gift of co-creation's goal
A self involved to complement the whole
In love's submission bravely to embark.
For though I have a will and mind to use,
Achievement pales when self and God can fuse.

FEBRUARY BUDS
For a dying student

Audacious February buds
broke early this year.
Woven webs
net winter-white skies,
pregnant branches shiver.
Impatient buds seek warmth
in sparrow-bodies
not in spring.

Sheltered from stirring wind
through windows I wonder,
was winter discontent
to wait for summer heat?
A day of promised sun
won't save February buds.
Snow clouds glower,
sour sap and juice
surfaced too soon.

Strange to see
one branch replete,
defying spring storms
forcing new leaves to fullness.
Snow-cold numbness
buries that branch
stifles life in progress.
Doing, being, promising,
these February buds wilt.

CRUCIBLE

"Have you got time to talk?"
Cold schoolroom lights
burn blue on brush-shined hair.
"I know you're busy
I won't stay long."
She sits.
Soft spring dress
printed pink and white
mocks her old young face.
I've seen it all before
filed with last year's lectures.
Thin fingers fidget on books
she could not read.
She masks her pain,
the kind that aches through eyes.
"I'm in trouble.
Please just listen."
The pattern recurs.
She talks it out
I nod and hear
hope to help
hurt to heal
but can't.

A plaguing vision: test tubes,
separate, sterile, strong
lurks behind my smile.
Imprisoned apart
we claw glass walls
muted by isolation.
"I know how you feel,"

echoes my tube,
but it's a lie.
Inside, an experiment
untouched by human hearts
she knows,
no one *can* understand.

CONTRASTING VIGNETTES

VACANT PERFECTION

The perfect lady
mincing, petite.
Self-importance balanced
on rose-tinted fingertips
delicately.
Proper inaction
allows no accidents.
Mind ordered
in precise cubby-holes
emptily furnished
without particles of dust
or thought.
Daily cleaning
polishes pettiness.
Practiced folded hands
hold nothing.

ALMA, LA CONTESSA

Velvet eyes search
three hundred years past.
New woman from a lost age,
antiquity reformed.
Five feet of energy
artist princess
Countess of joy
hop-scotching society.
Democratic idealism
wars inbred aristocracy.

ALMOST LIFE

Cindy was a pretty girl with plans.
University graduate,
she'd marry in June
know freedom and fullness
career and kids.
"There will be time."
She counted days
till she'd *begin.*
A few weeks more
of regimen and rites,
great expectations
till her almost-life
crashed with her car.

Ben was another.
"I'll start to live
after the dissertation."
He drank wine, looked weary.
"I'll be through next week."
He was.
Stealthy leak in his heart
ended another almost-life.

Almost-life:
Never shirk,
do your work,
wait till later to play--
or just to die
in almost-life?

CIRCLES TO CYCLES
in a meeting

Swimming greeny slime
words too thick to swallow
sloshing mushy slush
thoughts too flat to grasp
flaccid minds founder
undulating tongues
backstroke sludge.
Breathing's the problem
even athletes gasp.
We need fresh air
springtime's cycle
to end these circles
of confusion.
Leafy hope buds
in blades of grass:
Rain renews.

CONVENTION

A mind full of speeches
    translates
        A bellyful of bullshit

CLAUSTROPHOBIC

Time surrounds my mind
pressure on my head.
Trapped in the hourglass
I fight, confined.

Freedom contracts.
Grains of life
fill receding space
as sand deepens.

Just minutes left.
Can the curse reverse?
Will I escape at last
to floods of light and air?

Could glass walls fall?
Or will their closing trap
become my permanent urn,
crypt of final rest?

FLIGHT

Boardroom heat
smell of death
in baggy pinstripes.
Life's caricature:
Wizened forehead
maps emptiness.

Floating-above vision:
eagle perched
on eastern branch
the great Give-Away.
Spirit rejoins
Earth's force.

SEEING THE WORLD

GETTYSBURG REVISITED

Shining in the grass
on Cemetery Hill
on Little Roundtop
on Seminary Ridge,
careless monuments
to men long dead:
tossed beer can
or paper cup
or pink Kleenex
soggy and stained.
In the shop, a souvenir--
plastic bust of Lincoln
face in grim remorse
with prominent tag
"Made in China."
Bus tours crawl
through 35 curving miles
of Pennsylvania Piedmont--
Culp's Hill, Steven's Knoll.
Along the way, granite guides
chronicle the carnage:
On this knoll, 400 men perished.
Artillery roared, rifles cracked.
In three days of hell
51,000 soldiers died,
Lee's invasion crushed.
Is war ever worth this cost?
Then and now
Lincoln's "new birth of freedom"
unified nation, equality for all
still unrealized desire.
Hope barely breathes
in ragged patriot dreams.

HOOKED

From nickel slots
to high-stake roulette
the hook's the same
dream of wealth
the driver.

Tawdry casino
off the strip
din of slots
choke of smoke
dollars drop
in plastic cups.

Two in the morning
huge black woman
stumbles from the street
too drunk to know
snot runs on her face,
clothes reek from
days of "play."
Filthy washroom
stinks of vomit
as she squats
on a nasty stool.
It started as fun,
ended like this

Dream of wealth?
Money to gamble?
Life to waste?
The hook's the same.

THE MOURNING AFTER

The mourning after
When moving
makes windows weave
crazily
When closing one eye
stops hopping objects
but the bed revolves
When teeth and tongue
feel like someone else's
dry, sweet,
too big for your face

The mourning after
When insides turn out
When bruises turn blue
When floors feel lower
than yesterday
When you remember
a hundred dollar steak
that you can't remember
When soppy thought
sogs a pablum brain

The mourning after
you decide:
Waking for a wake
for the night before
isn't worth it anyway.

TROUBADOUR

Jackson Square New Orleans
Tourists gawk at human castoffs

One old man
grates out tunes,
skinny hands pluck
a dented tin guitar

> "Let's all get together
> while we can"

Torn shoe worn through
taps time on flagstone path
child-thin legs
quiver in grimy socks

> "Let's all shout together
> while we can"

White wooly hair wild
beneath his filthy cap
face contorted with song
or wine or junk

> "Let's all sing together
> while we can"

Teeth yellow against
brown leather face
with just the eyes
barely alive

"Let's all pray together
while we can"

Troubadour songs trouble and teach.
Some sing with empty heart.

NEW MEXICO IMAGE

Ceaseless winds
moan in telephone wires
sweep horizontal grit
over desert highways.
Flower fossils dry whole,
weeds curl, grass grays
in April's enduring chill.
Walk to the ridge
away from the road,
sterile hills layer
to the bleak horizon.
Expecting emptiness,
scattered huts surprise--
witness bygone times.
Abandoned stone hovels
honor survival in severity.
Six wizened trees,
two standing walls
act as stark sentinels
around the ruin.
Only the wind stirs,
whines across the rise
lonely for lost lives.

ON SCHEDULE

Crowded urban buses
belch and groan
rock on familiar rounds
carrying strangers.
Rigid rule:
Watch neon landmarks
store fronts and stoplights.
Look at your lap
or trash in the gutter,
but don't watch a person.
Glances can't meet
between city strangers.
Each one's alone
in space of his own
riding a bus
that follows its route
with uprooted cargo.

POLITICS

Thick sludge and muck
stirred with sticks of rhetoric.
Gummy, it clings to the mind
in sentencey lumps
fit to be washed away
by a clear, cold bath
of reason.

WATERCOLORS

Venus hangs low
in deep indigo.
Canyon walls
orange by day
fade to misty grey.
Restless breeze
curls beach grass
and tousled hair.
Fabled blue moon
silvers the calm lake,
black sky, quilted
with stars stitched
through wispy clouds.
Pale reflected light
laps the slippery hull
eased out from shore.
Campfire hurls
apricot puffballs
bright against the dark.
Your naked body
shines in starlight
fills me with rainbows.
When midnight sailors drift
hazy hues work
watercolor memories.

INSTRUCTORS

Seagulls
in dance perfection
soar sunward.
Effortless flight
slides from cloud to shore:
Beauty's book.

But on the beach
their raucous laughter
awkward caws
mark greedy scuffles
over ocean trash.

This is earth
our school in grace
presenting teachers.
More lessons will come.

MAZATLAN BEACH

Awed
by power, motion
compelling rush
relentless force
oddly reassured,
knowing this sea
owns us.

Beach sand shines
from brokenness.
Waves breaking
bring treasures
translucent shells
opalescent perfection
sea-life fragments
refined rock
broken tatters
all-color mix
formations of time
creation of motion.

Sit in sand
become this beach
washed clean
again, again
laved by love
part of the whole.
Waves engrave
nature's peace.

MAUI IMAGES

winter sun
    casts heavy nets
        catching clouds

        frozen water drop
            diamond rainbows dance
                as I shift my gaze

                pool-reflected sun
                    shimmers colors of surprise
                    promises of spring

∞

calm swan
    feeds to waterfall's edge
        then turns upstream

        frothy surf sound
            imitates meditation
                earth's breathing

                moist sea wind
                    kisses my hands
                    memory of love

∞

I touch the waves
    coming in white foam
        endlessly

        roiling surf
            clears my tracks
                utterly unimpressed

FANTASY

You're with me at last
in my quiet place.

Lovely London night
street noise below,
a walk in St. James,
Paris haze, Notre Dame,
showery day
beside the Seine,
fast train to Nice:
Private places of thought
beyond rituals.

You touched with me
Rodin's ecstatic *Kiss*,
smiled at the *Sculptor and his Muse*.
(You must recall
the nightfall wine, museum line
Rive Gauche rue,
Mediterranean view
we shared.)

Rows of roses
sweetened Marseille,
cut flowers
for all the tables of France.
Castles crumbled on distant peaks
hilltop shrines to a feudal past.

We were stunned by the glancing sea.
Purple bougainvillea draped
steep white cliffs rising
from sapphire waves.
Red-tiled villas in Cannes
primed poems dreamed
by mossy Venice canals.

Half a world away
in trains and planes
speeding foreignly
I held my fantasy,
together at last.

HOMECOMING

My map is old
but the world's still round.
I find my place
on the old globe,
North America, Colorado,
count time zones
turn the world eastward.
"Eight, nine, ten."
Red Sea, Saudi Arabia
half-way around the earth.
You're there, I'm here.

Your voice on the phone pauses.
Satellite delays disrupt.
My words, cut short
lose all I meant to say.

Fill empty time
with a new mantra—
I'm here for you.
Wales was a start
but ardor grows to love.

Soon you'll fly west
follow the sun
into your yesterday
my today.
Welcome home.

CABO SUNSET

The day seemed slow
till these last rich hours,
more precious as they pass.
Tasting their honey, I know:
this life rushed by,
incessant waves breaking
on eroding shores.
Doing, doing, doing
packing days like tragic plays
droning into night.

Breathing at last, I see!
New patterns unfold
like this tapestry of light
weaving its path
to the western horizon.
Fabric of solitude
fleeting but sweet,
being, being, being
nearly home.

FINISTERRA

Where the Sea of Cortez
marries the Pacific,
melding waters on this Sunday shore,
foamy tide climbs to its higher shelf,
washes my bare legs
erases footprints of earlier walkers.
A brilliant sun flexes muscles,
stronger here than in my mountain home.
This sensuous feast awakens every cell,
quickens my spirit to see
beyond mere eyes.

Walking to the point,
I admire precise herringbone patterns
drawn in the sand by the reaching tide.
Fluid fabric washes flat, then emerges again
as weaver waves retreat.
Abundant life! Shining out
like glints of sun dancing from here
to the flat line where sea meets sky.

This morning at daylight,
charter boats, armed with monster poles
to hook blue marlin,
paraded past this same beach,
converged at Cabo's pier
and swallowed macho warriors
who pay to kill.
Humbler fisher folk stand in the surf,
casting long lines
to reel in a writhing prize.
Mexican natives, simpler still,

work only with line, hook and weight,
clinging with bare feet to high granite
at the far end of the beach
stalking jack cavelle for tonight's table.

Smaller dramas play out at my feet.
Tiny crabs dig instant dens
Sucking sand behind them
in perfect round pits.
So many of them!
After a wave, the beach bubbles
like pudding in a pot,
pouring nutrients into blind mouths.

Another wave. Tiny mullet
wash up too far.
Stranded like driftwood,
wide eyes stare into space
as silver slivers flop and gasp
drowning in air.
Moved, I pick them up
toss them back
to their wet haven,
breathe easier myself.
But two large crabs scuttle past
into the fringe of foam
taking breakfast.
Token rescues don't matter--
creatures live their karma
to feed waiting crabs or flocking vultures
or other appropriate predators.
This is a beach buffet for true natives
and always has been.

I walk more slowly toward the point,
pondering fate.
Twenty feet from shore,
a lone pelican performs
his death-defying dive
crashing like kamikaze
to gulp his breakfast prey.

The point looms now.
Finisterra, land's end,
end of the earth.
What dark beast waits
in shadows of rocks
or smiles in innocent sunlight
to feast on this flesh?
What ocean of wisdom
will take me
and to what end?

Cabo San Lucas

WRITING LIFE

WHY WRITE?

Milk the moment
through lucid lens
poems to elude
the everyday
prose to plunge into it
turn abstract concrete
give the mute voice
tell truth
teach, learn
unearth surprise
become myself
because I must.

MAKING PEARLS

Consider the oyster . . .
Grinding, hurting
delving in depths of dark
exploring edges
transforming wounds
to work miracles
of beauty.

Poets also
grind and search
survey inner vacuums
discern obscure truth.
Familiar aloneness
taps uncharted nadir
unknown to others.
Bearer of world wounds
surrogate of woe
taster of ambrosia
echoing all,
creating.

ARTIST

Agile tightrope walker
    balances high, death below
        yawning endless jaws.

BLUESTOCKING LIMERICK

There was a bluestocking from Boulder
Who, past middle age grew bolder
She happily found
Her friends she'd astound
With verses quite hot (or colder).

OBITUARY
To Shelley and Keats

Pale flowers of another age
bleeding on the thorns of a life
long spent, how good
you wrote before now.
Scorned and exiled
you kept your dreams.
Your poems sang
climbing above your fears.

Today
dreams hardly live
visions falter:
Drugged in pollution
cremated in war
entombed in despair
our best minds, exploited,
create destruction.

Poems perish into prose
journalistic
to write the obituary
of our era.

POETIC DRIFT

hell fire shit & fuck
holler curse malign
the world is rotten
rolled in muck
it wallows in its slime

these words of poets
make it clear
read creeley plath and bly
you don't agree?
you're lost in fear
go screw yourself or die

you find a hope
you're called a dope
but speak your lonely view
you're not convinced
so try to cope
Wordsworth! where are you?

STITCHING A POEM

Pattern, scissors, thread, machine
whole cloth, folds smoothed,
latent beauty, flat and green.
Tissue-crinkled maps
pattern the adventure.
Parts appear to fit
but the fear of cutting!
Visions of couture grandeur
press the issue: I begin.
The pieces are all here,
to fit them together
is the problem.
Turn parts over, around
pin, baste, pray.
Sew, rip to sew again.
Bodice awry, skirt uneven.
Should it be shorter?
Fancy trim might help
but glitter looks cheap.
This material's sleazy--
or is it the seamstress?
Besides
My thread keeps breaking.
The machine skips.
Nothing fits.
I think I'll quit.
Never could sew anyway.

SHADOWS

Forest-laden air
color of star-glow
melts before me.
Stalking solitary shadows
light and dark mesh,
married in mind-flow.
Which is the shadow,
walker or shade?
the flesh or the dark
growing before me?
Cold now, wondering
how long is this walk?
Thoughts spin, words worn,
meaning can't be said.
Poem of no words--
shadows on the mind.

THE READING

"A poem should not mean, but be."
                    --Archibald MacLeish

Two poets on a weekend lark
agree: A reading for each other.
Next day, we sit prepared
poems copied, black on white, practiced.

I begin. But words I knew
turn strangers. Aliens.
From another writer? Another place?
I stumble on foreign language.

Next the words evolve to colors.
Tiny, fantastic tiles
glow across my page—
luminous hues beaming bright.

I try to keep "reading"
say what I see.
Again, the pages change,
lucid colors dazzle, defy words.

My eyes alone then
speak light,
brilliance beyond description:
Poem understood.

All talk ceases.
Sonia's gone now.
In the grassy park
she dances.

NEGLECTED MUSE

"Poets are only famous to each other."
"Five Elegies." Elizabeth Alexander

"Go!" he orders, "Care for her."
I skitter backwards, stumble.
The library door slams hard.
Designs of earlier days
carved in oaken banisters
steady halting steps.
Crimson carpet on downward stairs
dinges with mildew,
damp from leaked rain.
Uneasy now, I falter.
Seeing no one follows
I take the last step
peer through the cracked door
push into her shadowed space.
Her rumpled blanket reeks of neglect.
Dim light from a pale bulb
outlines a woman's round face
eyes dim, feverish,
dying in the dark.
Touched, I gather her frail body,
just in time
climb steep steps
toward the light.

ARTIST'S KALEIDOSCOPE

Mirroring fragments,
scattered odd pieces
of color and light,
the mystical, magical viewer
reveals, transforms
inspired patterns.
Healing brokenness into beauty,
connections appear,
touch, grow.
Fluid insights emerge
form, clarify.
Never static,
the kaleidoscope
opens new vistas
gathers shapes
warms the dark
illumines a dream.

TRANSITIONS

SISTERS

are sometimes found.
Strangers at first
awkward across a room
"Nice to meet you" grows to
"I know your heart."
Sister souls speak
unspoken words,
knowing.
An only child,
I have sisters
who pierce facades
melt cold loneliness.

They play my heart's song.
I choose my sisters
and sing along.

COYOTE WOMEN

Three nights now
coyotes on the hill
called me from sleep.
Hysterical laughter
from dark mountains
keeps the pack in touch.

Fresh kill
or just connection?

Tricksters, too,
we laugh in packs
reaching out, obscure
in the lonely dark.

THE WRECK

Wrenching recurring dream
shakes me again
wide-eyed, awake.

You drive fast
on a freeway west
eyes on your road ahead
no detours, destination clear.
Distant headlights loom
blue Jaguar juggernaut
bears down
speeding the opposite way.
Close now, it jerks left
crosses the line
too fast, head-on.
The crash comes.

Crippled by dread
I see it all,
powerless witness
the sole one standing.
I survey the ruins.
Blunt trauma to all,
one most serious.
Complicated head wounds
defy roadside diagnosis
unfurl slowly
alter life thereafter.
No one died
but no one escaped,
not even the bystander.

Rigid rejection
deep as divorce
was this blunt instrument.
No bloody bandages
covered this bludgeoning
but wounds went deep.
One wrong turn
caused the crash.
Friendship failed
when two turned away
hearts hardened,
sisters no more.

NOTE TO AN ABSENT HUSBAND

Bluish street lamps
glow in our bedroom glass.
Enough light to know
you're gone.
But I'd know without light—
Strange loudness of a ticking clock
Strange coldness of sheets on my arm
Strange emptiness beside me.
Even the children can't silence the need.
In their noise there is halfness.
I wish I'd told you that.
I wish I'd said . . .
But do you know?
In the dark,
do you also touch your ring
and remember?

VACATION

Miles of road
high mountainscape quiet—
Queer how quiet
with only two
after months of rush
office, deadlines, home and kids.
Droning motor lulls
rocks the mind.
"It's good to be alone," I said,
five hundred miles ago.
Alone. We are, you know,
All surface topics used
we founder, alone.
Not with each other
only inner voices make sense.
Alone together to learn
we're not together at all.
Quick! The radio!
Let jingle-ads-jangle-tunes
erase our jungle minds.
Hide loneliness with noise.
Thought seeps through silence.

MOOD

What's wrong?
Your distant look
chills
like the false notes
in your voice.
Your smile's a wall
I can't cry over.
We skim the top
of politeness.
My soul is sleet.
What's wrong?

THE FIGHT

Tough words
I can't unsay
stay in your flesh
drawing blood.
Like darts in your chest
I feel them in the dark.
"I'm sorry," I cry,
feel you nod
your arms reaching me
your warmth coming near.
Your body on mine
hints a hope.
But sharpness cuts
my own breast.
This wound we made
won't heal so fast
though that's a good try.

FROZEN

Frigid fog grips
quicksilver moon,
floating alone
in February gloom.
Misty cold corona,
embracing ice,
bitter as the wintry fear
chilling my numb mind.
Whining wind whispers
"You could die of this."

Belonging to Life
my threat
came too soon.
Not yet, Great Spirit!
Let me be awhile.
Enfold my soul
in warmer light,
till my Give-Away
is pure.

FRAGMENTATION

It's a way of life.
Broken dreams
plans, schemes.
Conflict liberates
doesn't heal.
Hearts stop.
Time splits into hours,
still minutes,
panicked seconds
intervene.
Bread is broken
also themes.
To break is to grow
to live is to know:
Sever, scatter, mend,
die and die again
to survive alive.

MISFIT

Lifetime trek
for lost belonging
soul-deep stretching
for faultless fit—
the room, street
mate, faith.
Each slip
loses ground.
Losses mount
as misfits wonder
Is home retrievable?

DEPRESSION

It's out gone out
my out/not in
black wick
dead glow
back no
black yes.
But
glow there
go there
stop.
Black wick
dead why?

NINTH DEATHS

Ninth deaths
are hard to recognize.
Rare cats play dead
sometimes
then Phoenix-like
rise and rise again
from cool ashes to warmth.
My cat seemed dead--
battered, bitter, beaten
looking life-lost.
But he rose.
And now I wonder:
Was the last death
his eighth?
How many more to go?

DAWNING

Alone in my bed
my husband and you
beside me
I fight it.
Watching the light
lick corners of the room
and curl around its sides
I close my eyes
to push away the dawn
that purrs against my cheek.
Hiding under breathing covers
I escape for a time
till relentless sun rises.
Another day to face
in contrived existence.

Now that I know
I'll always know.
Loving both
committed to one
this dawn's light
must spread.
This day must break
its honeyed ache
in words of dread.
"You'll only be hurt . . .
don't rack your dreams on me."

BUZZING FLY

Tapping on glass
beating tired wings
on adamant windows,
fresh-wind freedom
just outside this cage,
a fly tracks escape.

Wrapped in the room
drowning in words,
invent symbols
escape the drone,
tap a timid search
for cracks in my trap.

I hope we succeed.

IN-SIGHT

Surrounded by crowds

We're alone—

Our eyes touch.

GOOD MORNING

Prairie dawn
awakens Nature.
Apricot sunrise
warms etched cedars,
black on gold
greens slowly.
Tantalizing winds
wake wheatfield calm
stir scents of
dust and must.
Intense gaze exclaims!
Tentative touch
stirs senses
patiently expects
love.

OneSong

Cold night
crackled by fire-logs
other-where silent
lighted by shadows
between you and me.
Electric sensation
coming and coming
crying our oneness
needed and sweet.
Wine of my flesh
into your hands
I lay my body--
flawed
yet complete.

FOR TOMORROW

I'll kiss you a dream--
we'll speak in whispers
close our eyes
and see
symbolic yesterdays
glow into real tomorrows.

INTERRUPTIONS

I called
> Just a minute!

to say
> What's that?

what I meant
> Is it lost?

last night
> Can't you find it?

but couldn't.
> Look again.

You remember
> Try the bedroom.

how it was—
> Coming!

I have to say
> I won't be long.

I love you.

HOTEL

Five floors below,
traffic echoes
another goodbye.
A single rose blushes
with nighttime memory
fragrance of love.
Dark hours crawl
everything unclear
guilty secrets gall.
Two a.m. call comforts.
Distance fades
doubts recede.
Your voice sows
inventions of belief.
Drowsy warmth rides
cold winter light,
another day
another room
another hope.

APOLOGIA

So many words we hear to cut and hurt.
The world is harsh to smirk with devilish glee.
To listen is to faint from judgments curt
That taint the mind, exacting pensive fee.
"Adulterous cheat, unfaithful wife," they shout.
"You bear all blame, you own no good excuse."
I weep, protesting such unequal bout—
They might be right; I should give in, I muse.
But when I'm down, convinced I must be wrong,
I think of you, your smile and will so strong.
And when I listen, feeling ruined and weak,
I think of you, the gentle truths you speak.
And then I know the talking world is blind
To scorn, misunderstand my treasure find.

STORM WARNING

It's a lonely storm
when myselves conflict.
Blown from side to side
I can't decide
who wins
and either way
I lose.

PERFORMER

"Hurry! Hurry!
Curtain going up
See the lady bleed again
Twice a day
With a matinee."

Time after time
Practice perfected
Looking easy, hurting hard
It's moral, you know.
On with the show.

Costumed and masked
Typed and shaped
Accepted but sad
Cry aloud
To please the crowd.

MODERN PHOENIX

Strength gone
will weak
floating above
its mass of flesh
my soul stands watching.

From a space,
A death knell tolls.

Ashes before me
mute and cold
attest another fight fought
another struggle done
and won.

Ah, see,
A death knell tolls.

Winded and weary
body and spirit converge
weigh the cost of the fray.
Ashes affirm the deed:
Slain at last
life worried out
my dark beast.

Faint relief,
A death knell tolls.

My God, my God,
you have not forsaken me.
I sigh, thankful.
My sin is dead,
soul secure

Stinging joy—
A death knell tolls.

Yet what stirrings these
in warming ash?
What flame quickens?
What force is this
whose seed won't die?

My God, my God!
My flaming Phoenix
births anew
to war a weakened soul
a waning will.

Ominous now,
A death knell tolls.

RECKONING

Alone in echoing halls
listen for clues
in empty-building sounds
black-rain sighs.
Half afraid,
hurry to lighted rooms,
to face/ignore again
reminders of shame.
Pictures of the past
echo in lonely minds.
The night's too quiet.
Ask and ask
pray for reply
hear none.
God! Are ears deaf
or is there never/forever
forgiveness?

CONJUGAL FOOTNOTE

I am a one-note pipe
Playing my ordinary tune
Under the covers.

Grand opera surrounds me
With opulent options,
But the hero always dies.

In the twilight, listening to my breath,
I practice my instrument--
Unheard by all but one.

ON SEPARATION

Rootbound no more
my white violet
settles into fresh soil.
Old roots no longer fed
velvet stems, fragile blooms.
Leaves drooped, freshness faded,
constrained, it languished.

Total change required,
brutal blade cuts
horizontal roots
circling inner walls,
confinement slashed.

Wounded but vital
cut edges begin to grow.
Timid new roots
push tenderly past
outgrown patterns.
Boundaries fall,
rawness feeds renewal.

MID-LIFE

When I needed parties
people had to say
"You're okay."
Dress-face-mind
"acceptable."
Mask in place,
hope and fear
competed for control.

Now, I travel alone
liberated, at ease.
A quiet room,
evening glass of wine
enough, thanks.
Appearance manages
on its own
free just to be.

WARWICK DAWN

Icy English half-moon's
translucent tender light
slips into lacy fog
soft on the cheek of dawn.
Colors kiss these wintry eyes—
Tudor rose, edged in gold
turns grey to lighter pink
in virgin folds of clinging cloud.
Held close and safe
until the night
Moon's shyness relents,
welcomes the embrace
of Warwick's morning fog.
How can I say what I feel?
Transforming pain to hope
this glow begins a clearer day.
Mark this silver light.
Life has changed.

CHANNELING RESURRECTION

Nesting just north
of our open window,
lark greets light,
showers liquid silver
warbled song
across the garden.
Crystal notes cling
softly in space.
Rekindled joy
celebrates dawn.
Together, we practice
resurrection.

ANOTHER CHANCE

Startled from my solitude by the
slam of something against my window
I see with sorrow
a female robin, reeling crazily
swooping sideways to the nearest branch.
She clings to the cottonwood
teeters, then flails blindly
to the bank below.
Blood runs down the glass.
The deck below is spattered with it.
Shocked by sudden violence
I'm wrenched by her pain.
She flops on her back
helpless in the dry grass.
She's broken.

Another flash of flight:
Her mate lands beside her
a flurry of feathers
surer than she
hopping, flying, circling all around.
He lands, decisive, on her struggling form
takes her flailing wing in his beak
and lifts her up
rights her into a nesting pose.
Stunned, she rests on the hillside
motionless with her wounds.
I watch, enthralled.
The male waits,
protective sentinel.
She stays a long time.

Her restless partner leaves, returns
hovers with anxious attention.

She'll die, I think,
grieving innocent nature and
the cruel hardness of my civilized glass.
The raccoons will take her tonight.
But resurrection recurs.
When next I look
the battered robin is gone
somehow escaped from certain death
safe, I hope, in her own nest.

Celebrating in cold twilight, I ponder--
Without her mate
would she, today, have died alone?

MOUNTAIN HOME

MEDICINE WHEEL TURNING

I
Purification

SWEET GRASS

Braided sweet grass
hair of the earth
Mother-gift burns
sacred smoke.
Precious scent
celebrates memory
of Grandfathers returned.
Supple spirits bind
awaken, renew
in purifying rituals.
Sun Dance People
pronounce this medicine
good.

II
NORTH: Earth's resting and renewal

SWEAT LODGE

Oh Mother Earth
Oh Sister Moon
Help me walk straight,
Talk straight on the path of man.

Beckoning blackness
draws souls to

114

temples of life.
Hope fights fear,
silent confrontation
as the rug drops
hiding pre-dawn stars
closing breath into
womb-like space.
Steaming rocks
fill darkness
with heat and smoke,
Skin glistens wet,
thoughts purified.
The Medicine Way
moves to morning
the rug opens
again and again,
ceremonial greeting of
Great Spirit's works.
Dawn's light
freshens new eyes.

III
EAST: Preparation waking illumination

MEDICINE BAG

Red hawk soars
over greening slope,
muddy trails beckon.
Select symbols appear
in busy paths of fire mouse.
Emblems of relation
treasures of spirit:

hawk feather, cat hair
locust and aspen leaves
pine cone and columbine.
Earth signs hold
ancient wisdom.
Examined and mixed,
their soft leather bag
a microcosmic reminder
of mysterious paths
innocently entered
instantly understood:
patterns of kinship
freedom in nature
peaceful inscape.

IV
South: Growth harvesting trust

COLORADO RENAISSANCE

I will remember
high mountainscape rest
where pine needles
cushion a serene couch.
Patchy clouds
send frosty showers
to cool thirsty skin,
arouse drowsy
forest aroma.
Intense scent of pine
kisses my senses
as steady rain
nourishes the stream below.

Its sound profounds the quiet.
Lushness abounds—
columbine and iris
harebell and lupine
moss and lichen
and a thousand beauties
I cannot name.

In sweet silence
I welcome new life.
In and around
all is alive:
Colorado Renaissance.

V

West: Wisdom of mystical nature

CONNECTIONS

Fire rends the log
safely behind my screen.
Through glowing chinks
amid sooty bark
brilliant crevices
emblazon burning rifts,
flaring on darkness. .
Autumn nights invite
easy chair contemplation.
Time melts in this blaze.
Kee-Too-Wah trust
connects lives unknown.

Scent of river-rush
feeds Two-Feather's campfire.
Water striders skitter
in Bear Creek's still pool,
rippling unseen spirit dances.
Night air teaches
like a Grandfather,
touches Earth's heartbeat.
Illumined in firelight,
in mountain harmony
even stones are brothers.
This Winter Count
is a White Buffalo
moving to the North.

ZIA: VISION QUEST

Touching the earth
color of calm
you hear a quiet drum,
tale-spinner of silence.
Enigmatic mother,
I long to be with you
above words
spirit assured.
Lorekeeper,
guardian of legends,
what secrets hide
in folded hands, closed eyes?

(In shrinking pools
startled minnows flash
like shining shadows,
and in the burning fields
crack-lipped earth
cries for rain.)

Inscrutable face
vessel of wisdom
turn to this secret.
Does the sacred fire still burn
in these veins?
Will the blood survive?
I hear the drums
in lonely mountain places.
(Bring my roots rain.)

CHEROKEE BASKETS

Ancient hands,
worn with work
rutted with repetition
plait connections.

Green walnut hulls
darken split oak,
buckbrush strands
redden in bloodroot dyes.
Dry reeds
soften in water
to interlace
tribal designs--
    Chief's Daughter
    Man in a Coffin
Cherokee visions alive
in this alien time.

Wrinkled fingers
work the legacy--
honeysuckle runners
and bits of cane
form *Jacob's Ladder.*
Designs to bind
broken hearts to history.

SHADOW PATTERNS

Sun-showered hawk shadow
shies across the grass.
A butterfly flits, dips
meeting its own dark form
covered a moment
by dust-yellow wings.
Whirr of hummingbird
fleeting sound
here a moment, then gone.

Snowmelt, rockslide, talis—
patterns of nature
changing, changing
moving in time,
shadowy reflection
of growing thought:
nothing stands still.

FOOTHILLS SUNRISE

To the East,
lavender clouds
wisp into blue,
streaks of grey
blush to pink,
brilliant peach
deepens to orange.
To the West,
alpenglow gilds
sheer granite walls
fringed with shaded pines.
Rugged rocks shine!
Brisk gold flashes
on horizon's edge,
chill wind churns
black winter twigs
in eager welcome.
The rhapsody peaks
in rapturous dawn.

EVERGREEN

Sunday dawns
bright on autumn aspens.
Tender early light
quickens clarity.
Computer hum confines,
cozy walls close in.
Pull on jeans and boots,
escape to solitude
retreat to canyons
where bracing breezes
stir crisp October grass.

Cross and re-cross
dry Four-mile Creek.
Hop on river rocks
like the wary puma
hidden above.
Listen to silence
steep in sunshine--
alone but not lonely.

Down in the draw
a solitary pinion
kneels to the earth
in pose of devotion.
Needle-fingertips
reach for the far bank.
Bitter winter snows
nearly broke its back,
but not quite.

The miracle is
the tree didn't die.
Bent double,
scarred in submission,
its roots survived.
On the sun side, new limbs,
green arms stretched up
reaching for light.
A leader branch emerged fresh
re-birthed from roots of the old.

Surprised by joy
Alone, not lonely
Bent, not broken
Reborn
Ever green.

TRIFLES

Cloud fragments
puff and race
across midsummer's sun,
casting ephemeral shadows
on mindless pines
breathing fleet relief
from wringing heat.
Scudding shrouds soar
swell in importance
magnify a moment
condense, fly, flee,
drift and vanish.
Whiffing images of life.
graceful illusions of speed,
insubstantial vapors
strewn by wind's whim
connected to earth
only by the mind
of the sky-watcher.

VIELE LAKE VISIT

Preening for probable mates,
goslings now grown
show strange marks.
Pure white spots
scattered on throats
clash with feral green heads.
Speckled adolescents,
wild, yet domestic,
these half-breeds
vie for attention
disdain purebreds
force issues
defy convention
make statements
stand for principle
and shit on anything
that stands still.

SUN SAILING

Swallows sail
on streams of sunshine
high dive into deep sky
swoop through swells
circle and rise,
then pause by pinecones
bobbing on branches.

Diving off again
they swirl away
black wings paddling
rippled mountain breeze
to catch a current
and glide out of sight.

WINDPOEM

Gentle, calm or hushed
elusive and playful
stirring patterns in pools
with watery art

Changeable, whirling
aroused and stormy
darkness and lightening
electrified night

Destructive and fearsome
suddenly quiet
riding rainbows
submitting to sun

You dance with the weeds
welcome the summer
kiss all the flowers
left nodding behind

Never the same
always the same
invisible playmate
flighty friend.

SNOWSTORM

Our street wore its white coat today.
Houses shivered under bright furry caps
window eyes shining warm against the frost.
Swaying in sequined velvet,
pines matched the party mood
of children's eager songs.
Brown grass tried accessories--
soft scarves dappled pink and gold.
as the veiled sun cooled its light.
Blue and grey were the final choice
for earth's winter shawl.
She slept in muffled quiet,
dreaming of her new spring dress
put away for a warmer day.

SNOWY SKETCH

Quiet of the mountain,
time enough
to see winter
painted on the sky.
Tangible cold
wakes the senses,
calmed by muffled stillness.
Shrouded in white,
pine branches reach,
palms outstretched
catching fluffs of snow
to playfully fling
at a passing breeze.
Trees and rocks rest,
gray-black on a blanching sky,
all color stored till spring.
Tender evening light
etches leafless aspens
against a still horizon,
lacy sketches
created for peace.

VENEERS

Pristine snow, primitive cover
cools May's parturient bud.
Primeval shelter
shields the gravid branch
from wondering eyes.
Can new life survive
spring's constricting cold?
The old story retold:
Worry melts like ice
in shining rays
of a rising sun.

MARCH PROMISE

Emptying trash, I crunch
on snow thawing early.
Boots track watery dams
slipping on archaic ice.
An evensong staccato
drips from the weeping roof.
I fancy a face there
bearded, thin, *asking*.
The frozen sculpture
watches for spring
before falling in the night.

Moods change when
cold is limited to surfaces,
not bone and marrow.
Silken air reconciles
the argument.
In the distance
folded valleys hold moonlight
in softer, warmer hands.
I linger to breathe the breeze
watch pregnant pines waltz
against moon-melted clouds.
Sigh thanks. Inhale
earth's green promise.

MOUNTAIN THAW

Grey aspens crowd the hill
whisper no hint of green
though timid sun
offers hesitant promise.

Mountain wind stirs,
rumors life
in crusty grass.

Piney arms rouse
reach for high light,
warmer respite
from wistful winter.

Frozen fingers
of dry creek bed
point down the valley
where snow-clad edges
soften
and a tender thaw
finds it way
to the pond's icy heart.

NOTE TO A PREACHER

Sunday in the mountains
chapel at the camp
push the kids to church
just like home.
Ranger station religion
"Cancelled by Rain"
group sponsors stew,
plans askew.

Young faces shine.
liberated spirits
on new trails.
Washed by piney rain
senses cleansed
grateful awe awakens
visions of God--
sleek buttercups
cactus blossoms
sighing spruce
hummingbird whirr
wings a blur.

Streams speak.
Human words, artificial,
detract.
Earth is.

RETREAT

Butter sun delicate
hummingbird blur
movement dancing
cricket chirr
lonesome pine wind
petal sweet
mellow happiness
deep, yet fleet
pine needle shushing
narrow leaves
child cry quiet
mountain peace.

SLIVER OF SIGNIFICANCE

Scrambling up
this vertical path
felt foolish.
Too far to climb
to see again
a small wild strawberry.
It's lovely though—
rosy berry
flecked with gold,
bright leaves
velveted white
glowing against rock.
Unthinkable to pick it.
Here, it lives
under forest and sky
hidden from most eyes.
Only here is it real.
Down there, it would wilt
fresh color faded
tiny leaves dead.
It's good to know
this moment's beauty
in sacred silence.
What is essential?
Is life ever seen whole?
Or only in
slivers of significance?

STORM HOME

Space above hidden
shelter of spruce
shuts out the storm.
Roots are chairs
in this private house
soft moss a pillow
weathered bark, strong walls
low branches a fence.
Dry and quiet
we wait.
Nature's mood
merits awe.

CAMERA

How shall I save
these spots of time
to ungloom winter?
Can I leaf through thought
to live again
pictures I love most?

Translucent half-moon
caught on piney hilltop,
snow-shower whitening
bones of an old boomtown
cabins intact, though lives,
loves within are gone.
Rain touching my face
with green breeze
and deep-down freshness.
Tree-roof overhead,
mossy shelter
to ease a storm.
A doe
frightened out of sight
and hundreds of wildflowers
framing an aspen lake.
A waterfall picnic
one tiny mauve blossom
unique in all the world.
A broken stone,
its special shape
my keepsake.
River sound at night
and rain on the roof

while woodsmoke
cozies a cabin.
Wading an icy stream
to marvel at sunlight shimmer
through rain-studded pines.
Reading on the swinging bridge,
my chipmunk friend
visiting at twilight--
and spruce smell always.
My camera worked long
to snap sensuous moments,
vivid and sweet.
Enjoy the delights
of this memory album.
It belongs to you as well.

REMINDERS

Patches of old snow cling
under sentinel pines
so dense, green turns black
in shadows framing the river.
Under a pearl sky turning ice blue,
a beaver dam snags fallen limbs,
builds islands of debris
to defy the river's rush
with spring's cacophony.

On the hill, the aspen grove
wakes tender leaves, barely born,
delicate lace against May skies.
Studded white bark
blinks round black eyes
peering in all directions,
like stacked owls
watching for spring.

On the meadow below
shy wildflowers awake.
Tiny blue clusters
gather in fragile bouquets,
narrow pointed leaves
clinging to numinous Earth.
Warmer breezes pledge change,
Nature's rhythm assured.

Summer will come, then go,
fading into Colorado sunsets
like the light on the river,
like the forty years that fled
since we loved
mountain meadow toasts
rushing spring streams
young romantic dreams.

WHICH IS THE DREAM?

Shy small fireweed
rosy freshness plucked
pressed dry and flat,
leaves fading grey
in the wrong time and place.
Are you real?
Or is your only truth
on a mountain meadow
near rock and rushing falls?
Though I touch you now
are you just a dream,
ghost of a memorized moment?
I tried to save
this wee remembrance
to warm a winter's day.
Now I wonder
which is the dream—
now or then?

DESERT MIND

Sunburned shoulder of the hill
folded sandstone
wears afternoon sun
like a suede shawl.
Crack-lipped crevices
cry for rain
but empty white light
burns from the sky.
Hot horizons smolder
blistered and scorched,
obscuring vistas beyond.
This desert mind
withers, thirsting
in searing silence.

MEMORY ALBUM

Motoring across mountains,
four seasons in an afternoon's journey—
spring then winter then autumn gold,
with summer our hope for tomorrow.
Tentative rays through rain-veils
drive us faster to our river.
That river runs in my blood,
a journey to the Source.

Day breaks bright.
In the canoe
I savor glancing scenes,
sharp snapshots in my spirit album:

> *Gateways of sunshine*
> *open lowered clouds—*
> *river greens in new light.*

> *Sandstone, desert varnish*
> *flush in sun, retreat in shade.*

> *Millennial sculpture*
> *etches memories.*

Just around the bend
chattering rapids
speed heart, still thought.
I paddle past fast water
as river, canoe, and "I" merge.
Here, I'm most alive
feeling Earth-Mother's pulse

hearing her breath
inspired by palpable purity
cleansed of city-beat's
ordinary cares.

Shadows lengthen.
We camp, rest, dream.
Our day passes.
The river runs forever.

-- *Colorado River*

WHITE WATER

Canyon of solitude
in sunset hues,
walls of wonder couch
elastic air of pine-scent.
A throbbing pulse--
rushing lifeblood
courses this valley.
Beautiful torrent,
whisper, chatter,
sing of this stranger,
slipping through
your mighty home.
All is one.

CANYON WREN PRAYER

Gushing cadence
trills down the scale,
clear curved notes
carve silver songs,
wash red canyon walls.

Tawny tenor of desert cliffs
sing again to bless these stones
open this tired heart
soften edges
waken senses.

Oh rusty wren
raise your pure voice
speak for this pilgrim.
Sing thanks
for wild river roar
still evening peace.
Sing thanks.

--Colorado River

SUNSET TAPESTRY

The day seemed slow
till these last rich hours,
more precious as they pass.
Breathing freely now
fresh patterns unfold
in canyon tapestries of light.
A fleeting fabric of solitude
etches soft designs,
blesses this sandstone loom.

Here on this river
I know.
My time has rushed,
tumbled in incessant waves
breaking on eroding shores.
Constant rapids
chattered over rocks
drowned in swirling holes.

Paddling westward now
ripples unfold
in calmer waters.
The setting sun weaves
tranquil visions
on the western horizon,
flashing orange to softer gold
to quiet grey—
fabric of solitude,
colors of calm
wrapping me close
in night's soft embrace.

Canyon walls endure
water, wind, fire and time.
They stand still,
sunrise to sunset,
teach peace.

--Gunnison River

MANDALA WEST

Eastern tradition
widening circles,
concentric geometry
imaging wholeness.
How wide is the mandala?
My sphere holds
river rock lightening
the cat's curling purr
avalanche rush
apricot touch
folded valleys
trees on the sky
piney full moon
winter wind sigh
bower of warmth
whiskers on lace
dust smell.
Mandala:
Larger circles than before
opening.

QUIET TIME

Sitting like the Buddha
in Dominguez Canyon
I practice my heart's name,
grounded in rock and sky.
Profound silence is broken only
by river rush and canyon wren.

One-seed juniper lays shaded greens
on a dozen desert reds.
A distant totem guards this quiet,
enclosed by ancient sandstone walls.
By the stream below, miniature cottonwoods
try on autumn yellow
lighting the cloudy day like spots of sun.
Desert grasses dry to shades of gray,
the rusty earth textured by last night's rain.
All light is muted now
as earth holds her breath
waiting for winter.

The rock that bears my weight
hosts colonies of microscopic life,
creatures connected
as I am, to the whole--
all precious, all one.
In deep respect
I send lotus love to our home
and all who share it--
this heaven, this earth
this achingly beautiful life.

--Gunnison River

QUIETUDE

PAISLEY PATTERNS

lemon incense
rain-morning museums
an airedale's chocolate eyes
moon-wet mountaintops' fur-soft fog
brown-steam coffee   cement sidewalks
school rules   books   wrenched words
torn jeans   ice cream forgiveness
sport car freedom   acid rock   gin
thoreau   thurber   pizza perfume
woodsmoke stroking aspen air
bicycles   hiking boots
silver-satin sheets
sandalwood candle
sinsex   sermon
mushy cards
pineneedles
mozart   bly
wordsworth's I
forms in chaos
paisley patterns
life-poem

RELATIVITY

Science says the world is large
You must deem it otherwise.
Standing in your tiny spot
Contemplate and realize
Earth, to each, revolves on him
Round his joy, his want, his whim.
Life, to man, this knowledge gives:
Earth is small—a place he lives.

PHOTOGRAPHER

I see life through the lens
focused on bits,
clear images
of elemental details,
ecstatic empathy
with earth and sky
in minute views.
> *October snow cloaks a rose.*
> *Aspen twigs frame*
> *radiant thunderheads.*
> *Brook pebbles wink*
> *luminous luster.*
The whole overwhelms.
Meet reality close up,
epiphanies abound,
pointed by arrows of light
translucent unity
reflective insight
transcendent experience
clarified by intimate view.

DANDYLIGHT

Vibrant dandelion
turns a bright face
toward morning.
Insistent survivor,
point of light
shining nugget mined
from black depths of soil,
this perfect circle
echoes the sun
mirrors the earth
centers intersections
warms some old spirit.
Tired eyes caress
lush color,
welcome its certainty,
radiant light.

REFLECTIONS

Glassy water mirrors day's end,
sunset reflections rippled by
Canadian geese displaced.
Opalescent evening light
softens city cynic
walking edges
wondering how
we landed here.
In the stillness,
regal water mother
leads nine tiny copies,
heads bobbing
in rhythm with hers,
patterns of nature's renewal.
We share the evening
that begs a question:
Mother, teacher, mentor, friend,
what goslings swim in my wake?

AUTUMN LIGHT

Cleaning four-o'clock beds is a rite.
Summer's end, nod to autumn.
Crackling dry leaves fall together
with etched, mazelike designs
each unique in its scarred demise.
There is a brilliance in fall light.
Ideas come whole
like the last sweet raspberry
plucked by grimy gloves
from its sheltered place in the fence.
Aching poignancy of clear thought
burns with the flame of a maple.
Life is beautiful in autumn light:
bittersweet, understood
and short.

PRECIOUS MOMENTS

Warm as a lamp turned low
Sure as the seasons
Deep as springtime snow
True beyond reason

Soft as a rabbit's breath
Pure as lilac leaf
Loyal even to death
Clear as deep belief

Time with you shines
Fleet and sublime
Lark warble, breeze song
Precious moments, then gone!

AGE

A man, sere and gaunt
cold in his tattered hat
stands on the sidewalk
not moving, hardly breathing.
He waits, watching
parchment leaves
on winter oaks
cling to life.

Wintry man walks closer,
sad wisdom shading
eyes that see.
Reaching for a branch
he touches leaves
that wait uncertainly.

His frown deepens.
He would save these leaves
but can't.
High in the treetop
spring buds break,
the order of seasons set.
New life replaces old.
Every dry leaf falls to earth.

TRIBUTE

To Muriel Sibell Wolle

An old comrade
can be new.
Each day
open to risk
possibilities.
Free to choose
to learn
to teach
to love church
and Indian kids.
Countless friends
all grieve their loss
comforted by truth:
An arch-doer's
life begins
at the moment
called "death."

REMEDY

The silverware goes in first,
soaking in billows of bubbles.
I bathe each glass gently
wipe away lip prints,
attend to fork tines and spoons.
Washing dishes
somehow comforts.
Our little view of the world
framed by my kitchen window
seems safe inside the redwood fence,
tawny as piled autumn oak leaves
resting at its base.
Plates come next, pans last
shining wet in the suds.
I turn off the light, calmer.
Dear homely task
familiar and sure
muffles hollow echoes
in my mind.

GRANNY HIP-HOP

My head is aching
My ass is braking
My thoughts are taking
Too long to form.

My hair is graying
My strength's decaying
My mind is straying
Recalling youth.

But golden years
Are calm and dear
It's not too late
To contemplate
To heal all hate
And mend my fate.

My days are free
To just be me.

RETROSPECTION

Another Christmas season passed,
busy and predictable
ham and yams, green beans and pie
decoration on the door, glitter and glitz.
Tree ornaments, lovingly hung
radiate moving memories--
tiny wedding bell, 1961
first grade painted star
homemade trifles, knitted and stitched
trophies from trips, family gifts--
tender mementos of boys now men
dear ones gone, lives transformed
marriages, ended and begun.

What was certain, wasn't.
The impossible happened.
Shocks followed humdrum,
Christmases came and went,
wreaths hung, gifts given.
Time passed, prior life with it.

It happens this way.
Another tree, another feast
a year ends, another begins.
Taking down cherished baubles
we pack away the past,
out of sight but always present:
Ornaments and delusions,
keen reminders of all we were
when we thought we knew.

CONVERSION

Wildfires spread just over the ridge.
Eerie glow flashes on black
between mountain and sky.
Can we stay through this night?
Watch the flickering skyline and wait.
Evacuation looms till winds shift
and daylight seeps through haze.

I too came through fire
burning illusion to ash.
Now the wind has changed.
Today I commit to wake up, grow up
to take a right turn, a new name.
Buddhist. Pema. Lotus.

Ambiguity wilts in hope's heat.
Merging with reality
a solitary path opens.
Wildfires subside,
but this spark glows
vivid in my open heart.

GROWING THE LOTUS

As the moon sets in the West
strike the match, touch the wick
candle flickers, licks shadows.
Incense rises, senses awake.
The Buddha smiles, image of calm.
Strike the gong, mellow tone,
bow with inborn dignity.
Ancient ritual, familiar chants
mind prepared for peace.
On the cushion, erect, awake,
touch rising thought, let it go.
Fully present, sit in inner space.
Breath by breath, in and out
dissolve in the whole.
Day after day, learn to stay.
In shrine room hush, the lotus grows.
Born in the mud, it reaches for light.

CPSIA information can be obtained at www.ICGtesting.com
Printed in the USA
BVOW022140080712

294616BV00001B/13/P